Can the Orthodox Presbyterian Church Be Saved?

John W. Robbins

The Trinity Foundation

The Trinity Review

For though we walk in the flesh, we do not war according to the flesh, for the weapons of our warfare [are] not fleshly but mighty in God for pulling down strongholds, casting down arguments and every high thing that exalts itself against the knowledge of God, bringing every thought into captivity to the obedience of Christ. And they will be ready to punish all disobedience, when your obedience is fulfilled.

December 2004 – January 2005
Numbers 238 and 239

Published by
The Trinity Foundation
Post Office Box 68
Unicoi, Tennessee 37692
Website: http://www.trinityfoundation.org/
Telephone: 423.743.0199
Fax: 423.743.2005
Email: Jrob1517@aol.com

ISBN: 0-940931-67-2

Contents

By the same author:

Against the Churches: The Trinity Review 1989-1998 (author and editor)

Against the World: The Trinity Review 1978-1988 (author and editor)

Answer to Ayn Rand

Can the Orthodox Presbyterian Church Be Saved?

Christ and Civilization

The Church Effeminate (author and editor)

A Companion to The Current Justification Controversy

Cornelius Van Til: The Man and the Myth

Ecclesiastical Megalomania: The Economic and Political Thought of the Roman Catholic Church

Education, Christianity and the State (editor)

Essays on Ethics and Politics (editor)

God's Hammer: The Bible and Its Critics (editor)

Gordon H. Clark: Personal Recollections (author and editor)

A Man of Principle (author and editor)

Not Reformed at All: Medievalism in "Reformed" Churches

Pat Robertson: A Warning to America

Scripture Twisting in the Seminaries: Feminism

Without a Prayer: Ayn Rand and the Close of Her System

Can the Orthodox Presbyterian Church Be Saved?

DESPITE the painstaking efforts of many fine Christians within the Orthodox Presbyterian Church (OPC), the leaders of the OPC maintain a suicidal course. Despite the departure of congregations and individuals from the OPC, due to the leaders' collective inability to resolve the current justification controversy Biblically, the OPC leaders continue to advance doctrines that contradict Scripture. The OPC is, in the words of its late historian Charles Dennison, "obviously inept, bumbling, [and] confused."[1] That confusion now appears to be fatal.

The 2004 General Assembly

In an effort to clarify the confusion engendered by its decision in the Kinnaird case in 2003, the 2004 OPC General Assembly, consisting of about 135 commissioners (the denomination claims 28,000 members), voted, after some hesitation, to reaffirm the doctrine of justification as articulated in the 17th century Westminster Standards. Unfortunately, the 2004 General Assembly failed to say anything about the errors on the doctrine of salvation that some of its Teaching and Ruling Elders teach in the 21st century. In fact, according to its records, the 2004 General Assembly deleted language that referred to

1. Daniel E. Olinger and David K. Thompson, editors, *History for a Pilgrim People: The Historical Writings of Charles G. Dennison*. OPC, 2002, 208.

such errant teaching before passing the motion to repeat the language of the Westminster Standards on the doctrine of justification. The General Assembly apparently did not understand that when the Gospel is under attack in novel ways, rote reaffirmation of historic creeds is an expedient, but insufficient, response.

Such rote reaffirmation is insufficient because the signers of the Auburn Affirmation (1923/1924) wrote, "At the outset we affirm and declare our acceptance of the *Westminster Confession of Faith*, as we did at our ordinations, 'as containing the system of doctrine taught in the Holy Scriptures.' We sincerely hold and earnestly preach the doctrines of evangelical Christianity."[2] Rote reaffirmation is insufficient because the PCUSA affirmed the *Westminster Confession of Faith* for 30 years after it summarily suspended J. Gresham Machen from the ministry. Rote reaffirmation is insufficient because throughout the Shepherd controversy, from 1975 to 1982, Norman Shepherd insisted that he believed the *Westminster Confession of Faith* in general and justification by faith alone in particular. Rote reaffirmation is insufficient because, as O. Palmer Robertson pointed out, Norman Shepherd "could affirm that justification was 'by faith alone' and yet retain his position that justification was by faith and by works. For in his view the 'faith' that justifies is itself a work of obedience which is an integral aspect of the larger covenantal response of obedience for justification.... Even the classic assertion that justification is by 'faith alone' thus comes to mean that justification is by faith and by works...."[3]

2. See Edwin H. Rian, *The Presbyterian Conflict.* OPC [1940] 1992, 205.

3. O. Palmer Robertson, *The Current Justification Controversy.* The Trinity Foundation, 2003, 17. In October 2004 Norman Shepherd wrote a letter to *New Horizons* commending the OPC for reaffirming the *Westminster Confession* on justification, pointing out that some of the verses the OPC cited in its reaffirmation seem to support his views, and suggesting that the OPC also reaffirm other sections of the *Confession* that seem to support his views.

At this point in its history, the confessional affirmations of the OPC have no more credibility than the confessional affirmations of the PCUSA from 1936 to 1967. One of the commissioners to the 2004 OPC General Assembly made this very point: "There was a time when, if the OPC said it, it was accepted. The 2003 deliverance that accompanied the decision to acquit [John Kinnaird] destroyed forever that our words will not be questioned. The PCUSA always said that the [*Westminster*] *Confession* was their confession (even as they were denying it)." [4]

4. I am quoting the words contained in "Rev. Dr." Peter Wallace's account of the General Assembly, found at www.peterwallace.org/essays/GA2004. In his account, Wallace mentions John Robbins by name as a "schismatic" who "seceded from the PCA," and he laments that some people in the OPC are listening to schismatics like Robbins rather than to "the church."

Apparently Wallace does not know that a schismatic is someone who causes division by teaching doctrine contrary to Scripture: "Note those who cause divisions and offenses, contrary to the doctrine which you learned, and avoid them" (*Romans* 16:17). It is those who cause divisions and offenses by teaching contrary to Biblical doctrine, not those who are offended by false teaching, who are the schismatics. Many Presbyterian Elders, including Wallace, get the meaning of the word *schismatic* precisely backwards.

In 1927 J. Gresham Machen expressed his views on the subject of "schism": "Dr. [J. Ross] Stevenson [President of Princeton Seminary] objects to the League [of Evangelical Students] because it brings our students into connection with 'secession bodies,' with 'small institutions and sects which are committed to separation and secession....' I confess, gentlemen, that at no point is my disagreement with Dr. Stevenson more profound than here. His attitude at this point seems to me to be hostile to the very foundations of Christian liberty.... 'Forbid him not,' said our Lord, with regard to a secessionist of the early days, who was objected to because he did not follow with the company of the other disciples; and so from that day to this He has had in His care those who follow the dictates of their consciences in the worship and service of Him. We Protestants are all secessionists; and if, in the interests of organizational conformity, we fail to honor liberty of conscience, our high heritage has been lost" (quoted in Bradley J. Longfield, *The Presbyterian Controversy*. Oxford University Press, 1991, 52). To say, as "Rev. Dr." Wallace does, that leaving the PCA or the OPC is leaving "the Church of Jesus Christ" is to display ecclesiastical arrogance in keeping with that of the Roman Church-State and Wallace's Alma Mater, Notre Dame.

The same Commissioner said, "I am amazed that anyone [at the 2004 General Assembly] wants to bury this thing [an overture calling for reaffirmation of belief in justification by faith alone and the erection of a committee to study justification]. Everybody should be willing to do whatever is necessary that we may clarify this confusion." But almost half the General Assembly wanted to "bury this thing" and to refuse to consider the doctrine of justification. According to Peter Wallace's account of the General Assembly, the vote to find the overture in order almost failed, 68-64, and four men, all former moderators of the OPC General Assembly, asked that their negative votes be recorded: John Mahaffy, Thomas Tyson, Donald Duff, and Richard B. Gaffin, Jr. Subsequently the General Assembly elected a Committee to Study Justification, consisting of seven men, all of them seminary faculty members. Included on the Committee was Richard B. Gaffin, Jr. (who had voted against even considering the motion), senior member of the faculty at Westminster Seminary and one of the architects, with Norman Shepherd, of a new perspective on salvation that denies the Biblical doctrine of justification by faith alone.[5]

The OPC's record for the past 30 years on this central doctrine of the Christian faith is not good. It failed to condemn Norman Shepherd's teaching of justification by faith and works in the 1970s when it had opportunities to do so. In 2003 the General Assembly overturned John Kinnaird's conviction for teaching justification by faith and works, stating positively that his teaching was in accord with Scripture and the *Westminster Confession*. Some of the OPC's prominent Teaching Elders,

5. See Mark W. Karlberg, *The Changing of the Guard*. The Trinity Foundation, 2001; O. Palmer Robertson, *The Current Justification Controversy*. The Trinity Foundation, 2003; John W. Robbins, editor, *A Companion to The Current Justification Controversy*. The Trinity Foundation, 2003; and John Robbins and Sean Gerety, *Not Reformed at All: Medievalism in "Reformed" Churches*. The Trinity Foundation, 2004. The charge to the Committee to Study Justification does not mention Shepherd.

including Cornelius Van Til, John Frame (now in the PCA), and Richard B. Gaffin, Jr., have vocally defended Shepherd and his doctrine of justification.

This was not always so. When J. Gresham Machen and others started the OPC, then called the Presbyterian Church of America, in 1936, the stand of the Church for the Gospel was clear and consistent. But Machen was killed by overwork and pneumonia a few months later, and another institution he began, Westminster Seminary, a parachurch organization independent of and unsupervised by the OPC, first influenced and later controlled the denomination. The Seminary placed enough graduates in OPC congregations to shield their errant professors from criticism and discipline.

The OPC Magazine, *New Horizons*

One would expect the OPC to praise its principal founder J. Gresham Machen, or some of its other founders, such as Dr. Gordon H. Clark. But in the October 2004 issue of its denominational magazine, *New Horizons*, the OPC, instead of recalling its roots, published three articles praising Cornelius Van Til, who played no role in its founding. Even more ironically, the October 2004 issue of *New Horizons* is the "Reformation" issue. But Martin Luther and the Reformers got only a brief and obligatory mention (less than a paragraph) by the magazine's new editor, Danny Olinger, on page 2; and the Reformation was not mentioned again in the entire "Reformation" issue of the magazine. The doctrine of justification was not mentioned at all. The focus of *New Horizons* was on Van Til; the three longest articles were devoted to his praise. And one of the essays extolling Van Til, the one written by the official Historian of the OPC, spent some time criticizing Dr. Gordon Clark, one of the OPC's founders.

As a student at Princeton Seminary, Cornelius Van Til, reports William White in his authorized biography, was considered a "middle of the roader" by some of his fellow students in the Fundamentalist-Modernist controversy then raging within the seminary. After graduating from Princeton Seminary and University, Dr. Van Til took a pastorate in Spring Lake, Michigan, in the Christian Reformed Church. But he soon received a call to teach apologetics at Princeton Seminary, and he returned there in 1928. In 1929, when the General Assembly of the PCUSA appointed two signers of the Auburn Affirmation to the reorganized Princeton Seminary Board, four Princeton professors resigned: Gresham Machen, Robert Dick Wilson, Oswald Allis, and Cornelius Van Til. Van Til returned to Spring Lake, but Wilson, Allis, and Machen organized a new seminary. Other prominent Presbyterian pastors joined Machen's efforts, and four more men joined the faculty of the fledgling seminary: R. B. Kuiper, N. B. Stonehouse, Paul Woolley, and Allan MacRae. But Van Til stayed in Michigan. Westminster Seminary invited him to teach apologetics. He refused. Oswald Allis traveled to Michigan to speak to Van Til; Van Til still refused. Machen and Stonehouse went to visit him, and again he refused. Despite his familiarity with the transformation of Princeton Seminary into a modernist institution, Van Til did not share Machen's vision for a new seminary. (Van Til had taken no courses from Machen while he was at Princeton.) While others were eager to help Machen in his valiant defense of the faith, a defense that was to lead to his early death, Dr. Van Til was not. His biographer reports that one of the factors was his middle-of-the-roadism: "There was still another questionable feature about lining up with the Westminster [Seminary] men. Van Til had observed, while at Princeton, that some of the students intensely loyal to Machen and everything he represented, were loudly and disconcertingly argumentative. They did more harm to the cause than good, he often thought" (90). The irrationalism that characterized Van Til's entire philosophy can be seen in this one argument: Why should the deportment of some Princeton students (even if that were important, which it was not) affect his decision to help defend the faith by joining the faculty of the new seminary?

Dr. Van Til also remained in the Christian Reformed Church (CRC), even after many sound men had left it; and the Protestant Reformed Churches had pointed out some of the errors of the CRC in the 1920s and 1930s, errors that Van Til had in fact accepted. Because he was not Presbyterian, Van Til had not stood shoulder to shoulder with Machen in the battles of the 1920s and early 1930s. Unlike Machen or Dr. Clark, Van Til had never been a Presbyterian, and he played no noticeable role in the organization of the OPC. After the new church was organized, Van Til joined it, but he brought with him doctrinal baggage foreign to both Presbyterianism and Machen.

One man who did help Machen organize the OPC was Gordon Clark, but Ned Stonehouse, the biographer of Machen, did not mention Dr. Clark's role. So close was Dr. Clark to Machen, despite a 21-year difference in age, that he made the speech nominating Machen as the first moderator of the OPC at its first General Assembly, June 11, 1936. As the reader may have guessed, Machen's biographer, Dr. Stonehouse, was on the faculty of Westminster Seminary and was one of the opponents of Dr. Clark's doctrine and ordination.

The Controversy Continues

The current OPC Historian is John Muether of Reformed Theological Seminary, whose essay "Van Til the Controversialist" opens the October 2004 issue of *New Horizons*. In the course of his three-page essay on Van Til, Muether criticizes Gordon Clark repeatedly. On September 23, 2004, I wrote to Mr. Muether about his statements:

> In the latest issue of *New Horizons*, you make several statements about Gordon Clark that I would like more information about.

First, you make a passing reference to "false principles, whether the rationalism of Gordon Clark or the irrationalism of Karl Barth." What false principles, which you call rationalism, did Clark hold? Please provide quotations.

Second, you say that "Clark was a pawn in the agenda of a faction of the church that was discontent with its Reformed identity. Ultimately what was at stake was the question of whether the church's ecclesiology would be evangelical or Reformed."

I presume that as the OPC Historian, you have some documentary evidence that supports these statements. I would like to see those documents. Who were the members of this "faction"? How did they use Clark as a "pawn"? What was their "agenda"? How was their "discontent" with the "Reformed identity" of the OPC expressed? How did Clark become a "pawn," if, as is the case, the whole controversy began when the theological views of Clark were attacked by the Westminster faculty, which initiated the whole affair? Do you mean to suggest by your remarks that this whole controversy was at bottom not theological or doctrinal, but ecclesiastical? If so, why do you think that?

Third, you write, "But when the church rejected the agenda of broader evangelicalism, Clark and his supporters left the church." Again, what was this "agenda"? I would like to see some documentary evidence for it. Do you mean to suggest, as your words imply, that Clark was not Reformed, but "broadly evangelical"? What is the evidence for this? How did the church "reject" this "agenda of broader evangelicalism"? Was there a vote at GA?

Since you are the official Historian of the OPC, I hope I can anticipate a prompt, thorough, and accurate response to my requests for more information and documents supporting these statements, which are not supported in your essay.

Mr. Muether's response was disappointing. He did not provide any documents or quotations supporting his statements about Dr. Clark, but referred me to three other writers:

Dear Mr. Robbins,

1. Cornelius Van Til's claims about the rationalism of Gordon Clark can be found in his *Introduction to Systematic Theology* (1949), especially pages 16-17, 33, 37-38.

2. The broader ecclesiastical issues that accompanied the Clark debates in the Orthodox Presbyterian Church are well documented by Michael Hakkenberg ("The Battle over the Ordination of Gordon H. Clark," *Pressing Toward the Mark*, 329-50; see especially the "Program for Action" found in footnote 64 on pp. 349-50) and by Charles Dennison, *History for a Pilgrim People*, 131-35 (see esp. footnote 51 on p. 134).

Let us examine Mr. Muether's response and the sources he cites.

One of the characteristics of a competent historian is his practice of citing primary sources for his statements. If he makes an assertion about a person's views, for example, he quotes the words of that person. He does not merely quote or cite someone else, especially an opponent or critic of that person. In his first paragraph, Muether does not cite any words of Dr. Clark or any primary source; he cites only Van Til, perhaps Dr. Clark's most confused and determined opponent. This is not characteristic of a competent historian.

On pages 16-18 of Van Til's *An Introduction to Systematic Theology*, which Muether cites as supporting his accusation of "rationalism" against Dr. Clark, Van Til accuses Dr. Clark of both rationalism and irrationalism: He claims that Dr. Clark's view "assumes an irrationalist philosophy of fact" and that "Irrationalism is involved in rationalism and rationalism is involved in irrationalism" (18). Since Van Til in the context defines neither of these terms, they function merely as pious swear words. They are used only for their prejudicial, pejorative, and rhetorical effect; they have no scholarly, probative, or cognitive value whatsoever. The words Van Til actually quotes from Dr. Clark – such as this sentence from Dr. Clark's 1946 book, *A Christian Philosophy of Education*, "In view of this pragmatic dealing with history, its positivistic denial of universal law, of metaphysics, of supernatural interpretation, it may be permitted by way of anticipation to suggest the conclusion that, instead of beginning with facts and later discovering God, unless a thinker begins with God, he can never end with God, or get the facts either" – not only do not substantiate an accusation of either rationalism or irrationalism, they actually demonstrate Dr. Clark's presuppositionalism, *which Van Til attacks.* Van Til writes: "Now it is true that no Reformed person should begin with facts and later discover God, but it is equally true that no Reformed person should begin with God and later discover the facts" (17-18).[6] Van Til asserts that "every fact proves the existence of God" (17). After this sweeping assertion, Van Til fails to provide the proof.

Although Muether does not mention it, Van Til concludes this brief discussion of Dr. Clark's views by asserting his own view that there is no point of identity of content between God's mind and man's mind: "At no point does such a system [that, is, "Reformed confessions of faith"] pretend to state, point for point, the identical content of the original system of the mind of God.... To claim for the Christian system identity with the divine system at any point is to break the relationship of dependence of human knowledge on the divine will" (18-19). This second sentence is, of course, merely asserted; as with so much in Van Til's books, there is no Scriptural or other argument offered to support the assertion.

But what is more important to notice is Van Til's distinction between "the Christian system" and "the divine system." In Van Til's thought, there are two systems of theology, the

6. I am citing the 1971 edition of Van Til's *An Introduction to Systematic Theology*. It is "practically unaltered" (Van Til's words) from the 1946 edition, written during the Clark-Van Til controversy. Twenty-five years after the controversy, Van Til was still misrepresenting Dr. Clark's views to his students at Westminster Seminary, despite Dr. Clark's repeated requests to him to stop doing so.

"Christian system" and the "divine system." The "Christian system" is not the "divine system," and the "divine system" is not the "Christian system." Not only are the two systems different, they are completely different: There is no "identity of content" between them. Included in the "Christian system" are all Reformed confessions. According to Van Til, no Reformed confession does, or even can, claim to state the content of God's theological system "at any point." "At no point," Van Til writes, is there identical content in the Reformed confessions (the "Christian system") and the mind of God (the "divine system"). This utter agnosticism, this attack on Scripture and propositional revelation, this repudiation of all Reformed creeds and confessions *per se*, is compelling the OPC to commit theological suicide.[7]

The next citation from Van Til that Muether provides, page 33, is a discussion of the primacy of the intellect. It contains no quotations from Dr. Clark, and no accusation of "rationalism."

The third and final citation Muether provides from Van Til is pages 37 and 38. They also contain no mention of Dr. Clark. Page 39 mentions Dr. Clark in passing, who, Van Til says, "appeal[s] constantly to the abstract principle of contradiction for the defense of the Christian position." That, apparently, is wrong. Pointing out that non-Christian views contradict themselves is somehow illegitimate in apologetics. But Van Til makes no accusation of rationalism on this page either.

To recapitulate, the OPC Historian, John Muether, failed to substantiate his assertion that Dr. Clark taught something called the "false principles" of "rationalism" that were opposed to Christianity. Specifically, Muether failed to answer my

7. For one source of this Antichristian agnosticism, see the first 25 or so pages of Herman Bavinck's *The Doctrine of God*. They are a sustained attack on propositional revelation. I quote a few sentences from Bavinck on page 36.

simple request: "What false principles, which you call rationalism, did Clark hold? Please provide quotations." Muether provided no quotations. His citations of Van Til were equally empty. In fact, there are no such quotations to be found in Dr. Clark's books, and the accusation of holding the "false principles" of "rationalism" is a slander against Dr. Clark that Van Tilians have been repeating for decades in both their official and private communications. Nearly twenty years after his death, both the official Historian and the official magazine of the OPC find it necessary to continue their smear campaign against Gordon Clark.

Let us move on to the second part of my request to Mr. Muether for documentation of his statements.

Muether again, rather than citing original sources, cites two writers, Michael Hakkenberg and Charles Dennison, his predecessor as OPC Historian.[8] Let us take Hakkenberg first.[9]

In the semi-centennial volume celebrating the OPC, *Pressing Toward the Mark*, Hakkenberg characterized the Clark-Van Til controversy as one arising out of a concern for "doctrinal purity," but said that it would be "misleading to suppose that strictly doctrinal issues were involved" (330). I think Hakkenberg was quite mistaken in his first remark and quite correct in his latter statement. As we shall see, the Westminster faculty apparently feared that the Seminary, an independent parachurch organization that supplied many of the Teaching Elders to the OPC, would come under the oversight of the

8. Charles Dennison studied at Duquesne University and at Westminster Theological Seminary under Richard B. Gaffin, Jr., Cornelius Van Til, and Meredith Kline. He served as pastor of Grace Orthodox Presbyterian Church in Sewickley, Pennsylvania, from 1976 to 1999, and as Historian of the OPC from 1981-1999. Tragically, Mr. Dennison died in April 1999.

9. At the time he wrote his essay, Hakkenberg was a member of the Christian Reformed Church and a doctoral candidate at the University of California at Berkeley. He has since received his doctorate and teaches at Roanoke College in Virginia.

Church, thus losing its independence.[10] There was also the possibility that if Dr. Clark were ordained a Teaching Elder (he was already ordained a Ruling Elder), and the Seminary came under the oversight of the Church, the Church might name Dr. Clark to the Seminary faculty. After all, Dr. Clark's connections to Machen were well-known at that time; he was a founding Elder of the OPC; and his theological and academic credentials were exemplary.

Hakkenberg wrote: "Clark and a number of other ministers left the OPC over seemingly non-fundamental and highly technical doctrinal matters, since on the surface it seems as though the theological issues involved should not have warranted such an extreme action"(330). Hakkenberg apparently forgot that the Westminster Seminary faculty had sought to defrock Dr. Clark, not by charging him judicially with doctrinal error and so affording him the protection of due process, but by administrative action. (This was the same tactic the PCUSA had used against Machen a decade earlier.) Moreover,

10. In *The Current Justification Controversy*, O. Palmer Robertson shows how the Seminary faculty and President Clowney used their independence from the OPC to shield Norman Shepherd from Church discipline. When charges were filed against Shepherd in the Philadelphia Presbytery of the OPC in 1977, the Seminary, which dominated the Presbytery, argued that evidence against Shepherd ought to be suppressed, and the Presbytery, persuaded by specious arguments about academic freedom, agreed. Robertson writes: "the Presbytery relinquished its right of supervision over one of it own ministers. In effect, the academic community of the Seminary was judged by Presbytery to possess a right of supervision over its ministers that was above its own. By refusing to look at the documents themselves, the Presbytery allowed a majority of the Seminary faculty to determine when the theological expressions of a minister were to be regarded as 'experimental' and 'academic,' without reviewing the substance of the question itself" (32-33). The OPC, in particular the Philadelphia Presbytery, was dominated by the Van Tilian Westminster faculty during the Clark controversy, and 30 years later it still dominated during the Shepherd controversy and short-circuited all discipline of Shepherd for his heretical teachings. Van Til even showed up on the floor of the Philadelphia Presbytery and defended Shepherd's heresies, with John Frame's help.

Hakkenberg's misreading of the situation created a pseudo-problem that required him to impute ulterior motives to Dr. Clark's defenders. Hakkenberg's interpretation also implied, which I am sure he did not mean to imply, that the Westminster Seminary faculty had attacked Dr. Clark over "seemingly non-fundamental and highly technical doctrinal matters." The Seminary faction had not only initiated the attack on Dr. Clark, but it had sustained the attack for years over what Hakkenberg described as relatively unimportant matters.

Let me be clear on this: There is no evidence, and neither Muether, Dennison, nor Hakkenberg cited any, that Dr. Clark and those who later defended him from the Westminster Theological Seminary (WTS) faction in the OPC started the Clark-Van Til controversy. Van Til and the WTS faction launched an unprovoked attack on Dr. Clark in 1943 when he sought ordination in the Philadelphia Presbytery. Prior to this attack, Dr. Clark had been on good terms with Westminster, so far as he knew. Dr. Clark had been the commencement speaker at Westminster Seminary in 1941. *(The Trinity Review* reprinted that commencement address, "A Protestant Worldview," in one of its early issues.) As Chairman of the Department of Philosophy at Wheaton College from 1936 to 1943, Dr. Clark had steered many aspiring ministers to Westminster for their theological education. Edward L. Kellogg (who was one of the Complainants against Dr. Clark's ordination in 1944), in the same volume in which Hakkenberg's essay appears, *Pressing Toward the Mark*, reported that "a sizable percentage of the student body in the early years of Westminster consisted of students who came from Wheaton" (446). Kellogg did not mention Dr. Clark's role in this; in fact Kellogg did not even mention Dr. Clark's name. Ironically, Kellogg attributed the influx of Wheaton students to J. Oliver Buswell, Jr., who, initially an ally of Machen, quickly developed serious disagreements with Machen, left the OPC in 1937, and became moderator of the new Bible Presbyterian Church in 1938.

Fortunately there were other witnesses who have no anti-Clark axe to grind. For example, Dr. William Young, Chairman of the Department of Philosophy at the University of Rhode Island, later wrote, "At Westminster Seminary in the year 1939-1940, I recall that the junior class, including President Clowney, was overwhelmingly the result of Dr. Clark's Creed Club and Calvinistic teaching at Wheaton College."[11]

The Westminster Seminary faculty picked the fight with Dr. Clark and chose the grounds on which they wished to oppose him. Dr. Clark did not initiate the controversy, and he did not choose those grounds. Hakkenberg's characterization of the issues as unimportant implies that the Seminary faculty, unable to find any serious error with which to charge Dr. Clark, chose to raise "non-fundamental and highly technical" matters. Moreover, since the controversy lasted for years, Hakkenberg's analysis implies that the Seminary faculty stubbornly refused to restore the peace of the church by dropping its "non-fundamental and highly technical" arguments against Dr. Clark. This was done, at least in part, for non-doctrinal reasons, according to Hakkenberg. I have already noted what those reasons were: fear that WTS would become subject to the oversight of the OPC, and that Dr. Clark might be named by the OPC to the faculty of the Seminary, were he ordained a Teaching Elder. Dr. Robert Rudolf reported that "Dr. Van Til said that Clark was probably the most effective teacher he knew and therefore he was afraid of the great influence he would have on students...."[12]

Later in his essay, Hakkenberg discloses the real reasons that led to Dr. Clark's departure from the OPC: "However, because of the constant and often bitter opposition to his ordination Clark left the denomination that same year [1948]"

11. William Young, "Absolute Truth," in *Gordon H. Clark: Personal Recollections*, John W. Robbins, editor. The Trinity Foundation, 1987, 115.

12. "A Truly Great and Brilliant Friend," in *Gordon H. Clark: Personal Recollections*, 104.

(336). The WTS faction disrupted the peace and purity of the OPC for years; it maintained its campaign of misrepresentation and innuendo against Dr. Clark; and it feared that if the Seminary were to be supervised by the Church it would lose its autonomy. It was this vicious campaign that led to Dr. Clark's departure from the OPC. Today the anti-Clark-pro-Van Til climate is so heavy in the OPC that a minister who expressed his preference for Clark and doubt about Van Til would face the same sort of campaign that drove Dr. Clark and his defenders from the denomination in 1948.

In his *New Horizons* essay, OPC Historian Muether said that the WTS faction was defending "Reformed ecclesiology." Hardly. The WTS faction opposed Reformed ecclesiology and defended the independent, parachurch status of Westminster Seminary, which was its power base in controlling the OPC.

Hakkenberg wrote: "A Reformed theology, although important to this group [the "Clark group"] was not crucial in the battle against modernism" (337). Hakkenberg cited no source for this statement, no quotation, not even a sentence, from any member of this "group," let alone from the whole group. Hakkenberg repeatedly referred to "Clark's willingness to cooperate with fundamentalists in the battle against modernism," falsely implying that Dr. Clark was willing to water down Reformed theology in order to achieve such cooperation. Hakkenberg suggested that this willingness to cooperate with Fundamentalists in the battle against Modernism (which was a policy that Machen had in fact pursued), led Van Til and his supporters to "suspect" that Dr. Clark's theology was "not Reformed enough and perhaps Arminian" (337). That suspicion was, of course, complete speculation, without any basis in fact, and neither the WTS faction nor Hakkenberg, nor any official OPC Historian, writing 40 or more years later, supplied any evidence for it. But there was and is plenty of evidence against it.

"An Appeal to Fundamentalists"

In March 1943 Dr. Clark had published an essay in *The Presbyterian Guardian* titled "An Appeal to Fundamentalists." Here is what he wrote:

> Whenever the late Dr. J. Gresham Machen was confronted with the opposition between Modernism and Fundamentalism, he always made it clear that he was a Fundamentalist. The term, be believed, was not sufficiently specific, but the disjunction was clear-cut and his stand was unambiguous. He was a Bible-believing Christian....
>
> First of all, let us look at fundamentalist performance in the last twenty years. As Modernism made inroads in the larger denominations, small groups of Fundamentalists here and there became disgusted and, rather than take up the disagreeable task of fighting for the purity of their denominations, quietly withdrew to form independent Bible churches. Some, not willing even to withdraw, simply closed their eyes to the denominational situation and quietly went to sleep in the false security of their local congregations.
>
> Both courses of action injured the cause of Christ, and in several ways. The withdrawal of Bible-believing Christians from the denominations made the progress of Modernism all the easier, so that when some noble men, like Dr. Machen, attempted to resist infidelity in the church, not only were false charges brought against them, but also they were tried and condemned in the ecclesiastical courts without being given the simple justice of a hearing – without being permitted to present their defense.
>
> In the second place, the formation of independent churches effectively prevented these Bible-believing Christians from forming a compact body for the united and aggressive extension of the gospel. They became disorganized remnants of a once-great army, powerless before organized unbelief. After twenty years of work, or at least of existence, the independent leaders of Fundamentalism have not accomplished the task set for them by the men of 1912 [the writers of *The Fundamentals*].

Nor can these leaders point with pride to the quality of the Christianity they have fostered – if quality is to be substituted for quantity. That real Christians are proportionally fewer today than twenty years ago is not a fact lightly to be laughed off; but some comfort could have been generated if there had been an improving quality to compensate. But at this point, too, these leaders have surrendered to the enemy and have betrayed their people.... Thus their belief in the inerrancy of Holy Scripture was rendered impotent by their neglect of so much of its content.

The result of such leadership is that many of these independent churches today can hardly be called truly fundamental.... But because for the last twenty years they [the people in these churches] have never heard of many of the very important doctrines, these poor people have been raised from childhood in ignorance of blessed and profound truths that God has revealed to us for our edification. Because their ministers have neglected to instruct them in the whole counsel of God, they are blown about, not by every wind of doctrine, but at least by many winds. In some places the doctrine of grace is vitiated by assigning a part of salvation to man's efforts, so that irresistible grace is replaced by the doctrine of free will as taught in the Romish church. Furthermore, some Fundamentalists are preaching that there are several ways of salvation. One was for this age and other ways for other ages....

But let us rather ask what Bible-believing Christians need.

First of all, the scattered, independent congregations of devout and humble Christians need ministers who have renewed their grip on the fundamentals. Both ministers and people should take Charles Hodge off the shelf and learn what the deity of Christ, the atonement, the person and work of the Holy Ghost, really mean. Next, the ministers should lead the way beyond the fundamentals to the essentials: total depravity and its implications, unconditional election, and irresistible grace. In short, he should possess himself of all the doctrines of the original Reformers. A close study of Calvin's *Institutes* and the confessions of the Reformed churches would be a big step toward the recovery of a lost heritage. Then when

> faithful preaching gives the people a fair understanding of these divine truths, the prospects of the church of Christ will look bright indeed.
>
> Finally, these leaders should cease their defeatist independentism and get back to the Scriptural principles of cohesion among congregations. The apostolic churches were united and sent delegates to a general council in Jerusalem. America can do well without one big antichristian Protestant church, but it desperately needs well-organized, aggressive denominations true to the whole counsel of God. Disorganized, independent congregations with abbreviated creeds stand in pitiful contrast with the appalling situation of the day.
>
> And if the present leaders of independent Fundamentalism are unable or unwilling to follow the principles of the Scripture they acknowledge, the common people themselves must seek a better leadership in a sound, aggressive denomination that not only acknowledges the Bible but also preaches it in its entirety.
>
> In very plain words, we invite you to unite with us, The Orthodox Presbyterian Church.

Anyone of sound mind who read this 1943 essay would not have suspected Dr. Clark of doctrinal indifference, willingness to compromise, Arminianism, or disloyalty to the Reformed faith and to the OPC. Only someone with an animus against Dr. Clark could so deliberately misconstrue his views. This essay was not only easily available to the WTS faction at the time, but also to Charles Dennison, John Muether, and Michael Hakkenberg 40 years later. John Muether and D. G. Hart, in their OPC book *Fighting the Good Fight: A Brief History of the Orthodox Presbyterian Church*, characterized Dr. Clark's 1943 essay in these words:

> Clark and his supporters wanted the OPC to join forces with other conservatives in the United States. The basis for this union was not the explicitly Reformed views of the Westminster faculty but rather the broad mission of opposing modernism and banding together for effective outreach. In

> 1943 Clark went so far as to invite all foes of liberalism to join the OPC. Ministers in the OPC who sided with Clark also hoped the church would become more evangelical than Reformed.[13]

Hart-and-Muether's statements are patently false. They misrepresent Dr. Clark's 1943 essay as compromising, disloyal to both the Reformed faith and the OPC. They know better. And as the reader now knows as well, Dr. Clark actually invited fundamentalists to leave their impotent, independent congregations, their truncated view of Christianity, and their leaders who were leading them astray, and to join a "sound, aggressive denomination" that, at that time, "preached the Bible in its entirety." He even urged them to study Charles Hodge's three-volume *Systematic Theology*. The *basis* of their joining the OPC[14] was not the broad mission of opposing Modernism, as Hart and Muether say, but "all the doctrines of the original Reformers," as one can easily see by reading Dr. Clark's essay. The *purpose* or *goal* of asking fundamentalists to join the OPC was to oppose all forms of unbelief, including Modernism.

Further, notice that Hart and Muether do not make the *Westminster Confession* the standard of Reformed orthodoxy, but, "the explicitly Reformed views of the Westminster faculty." In their minds, the views of the WTS faculty were the true standard of orthodoxy, not the *Westminster Confession of Faith*. Van Til's peculiar and erroneous views were made the test of orthodoxy in the OPC in the 1940s, and the official Historians of the OPC defend that policy to this day.

13. D. G. Hart and John Muether, *Fighting the Good Fight: A Brief History of the Orthodox Presbyterian Church*. OPC, 1995, 117.

14. The misleading language of Hart and Muether may also be seen in that they refer to the OPC "join[ing] forces with other conservatives," and to "this union," as though Dr. Clark had proposed the merger of the OPC with some fundamentalist group, rather than maintaining its own separate and Reformed identity.

Moreover, Hart-and-Muether's statement that "ministers in the OPC who sided with Clark also hoped the church would become more evangelical than Reformed" is doubly false. First, Hart and Muether cite no evidence that supports this allegation; and second, their word "also" suggests that Dr. Clark "hoped the church would become more evangelical than Reformed." Nothing could be further from the truth, as shown by Dr. Clark's 1943 essay. Like the WTS faction, Muether and Hart can find nothing with which to charge Dr. Clark, so they are reduced to misrepresenting his views.[15]

But the problem goes deeper than misrepresentation of one essay by Dr. Clark. The official OPC spin on the Clark-Van Til controversy is that the WTS faculty, whose views were made the standard of orthodoxy, were defending the church against the "broad evangelicalism" of Gordon Clark. They cite no evidence to support such an interpretation, and I cite evidence to contradict it. So why do they say it? There is a reason, not a good one, but a reason nonetheless: The official Historians of the OPC do not write history, but propaganda designed to cover up the reprehensible behavior of Van Til and the entire WTS faction in attacking a man of sterling academic, theological, and ecclesiastical credentials. Rather than admitting that Dr. Clark was not broadly evangelical and did not seek any compromise with Arminians, rather than reporting that Dr. Clark was in fact a strict adherent to the *Westminster Confession of Faith,* an enthusiastic supporter of J. Gresham Machen, and a founding Elder of the OPC, the OPC Historians have concocted a version of the controversy that bears little resemblance to the truth. Hart and Muether conclude, "In sum, Dr. Clark failed to express unequivocally

15. It is telling that there is no mention of the Shepherd controversy in this book of 200 pages that purports to be a history of the OPC. As Mark Karlberg commented: "It is a chapter in the history of the denomination and the Seminary some would prefer to forget – or possibly erase from the historical record, were that possible" (*The Changing of the Guard,* 37n28).

a God-centered understanding of the Christian religion."[16] They cite no evidence to support this falsehood.

In their history of the OPC, Hart and Muether cannot even get simple facts about Dr. Clark correct. They falsely report, for example, that "He [Clark] was licensed to preach and ordained at the same meeting."[17] They seem to be confusing John Murray's ordination and licensure with Dr. Clark's, for Murray had in fact been examined, licensed, and ordained all in one day, May 28, 1937. Dr. Clark was initially examined in early 1943, examined again and passed for licensure March 20, 1944, actually licensed July 7, 1944, and ordained in August 1944, over a period of about 15 months. Ironically, the procedural complaint that the WTS faction brought against the Presbytery of Philadelphia was its undue haste in ordaining Dr. Clark. Apparently one day is fine, if the subject is John Murray; but fifteen months is too hasty, if the subject is Gordon Clark.

The OPC itself pointed out in its 2001 publication, *What Is the OPC? Basic Information to Acquaint You with the Orthodox Presbyterian Church*, the founders of the OPC (which of course include Dr. Clark), "hoped that a mass exodus of Bible-believing Christians would swell the ranks of the new denomination, but it never happened" (4). Dr. Clark obviously still held out that hope in 1943, for which he was then and still is accused of compromise and Arminianism by the supporters of Van Til and the WTS faction. How far that accusation is from being true, and how slanderous that accusation is, can be seen not only in his subsequent books, but in the fact that in 1943 Dr. Clark was removed from his position as Chairman of the Department of Philosophy at Wheaton College because of his thoroughgoing and uncompromising Calvinism.[18]

16. *Fighting the Good Fight*, 114.

17. *Fighting the Good Fight*, 107.

18. See *Gordon H. Clark: Personal Recollections, passim.* After his 1961 book *Religion, Reason and Revelation* appeared, J. Oliver Buswell, Jr., writ-

But by 1945 Dr. Clark had realized that the OPC was abandoning Machen's vision and had "assumed the position of an isolationist porcupine." "We are no longer fighting shoulder to shoulder with other Bible-believing Christians," he wrote in the *Presbyterian Guardian* in 1945. "We have changed.... The customs, procedures and temperament of American Presbyterianism are in certain quarters [of the OPC] matters of disparagement.... Instead of leading the Christian forces of our country, we have assumed the position of an isolationist porcupine." Machen's dream was dying, if not dead.

Dr. Clark's leaving the OPC was not due to his failure to prevail in the Clark-Van Til controversy, for he did prevail. His ordination was upheld by the OPC General Assembly. Dr. Clark and his defenders left the OPC because the WTS faction, controlling the committee with jurisdiction over the matter, almost immediately after they had been defeated in the Clark case, refused to approve Floyd Hamilton's call to teach in a Korean Presbyterian seminary. Hamilton was a veteran missionary to Korea, but because he had agreed with Dr. Clark and not Van Til, the WTS faction used its clout in committee to thwart his call to Korea. This action indicated that the WTS faction, despite its "apology" to the Church for its sinful behavior in the Clark case, was incorrigible, and intended to disrupt the peace of the Church for another four years, if necessary. Dr. Clark's defenders thought their time and energy were better spent in proclaiming the Gospel than in fighting stubborn academics who postured as the sole defenders of the Reformed faith, opposed a "sound, aggressive denomination," and congratulated themselves on their "purity," a "purity" that

---

ing in the November 1962 issue of the *Evangelical Presbyterian Reporter*, attacked Dr. Clark's Calvinism as too "brittle" for him. Buswell expressed his especial distaste for Dr. Clark's "rigid determinism." Buswell was, of course, president of Wheaton until 1940 and later president of Covenant Seminary.

has driven the denomination to the brink of apostasy. Years later Dr. Clark told me that he would have preferred to stay in the OPC, defeat the Westminster faculty again, and restore the OPC to the ideals it had when J. Gresham Machen was alive. Obviously he could not do that alone, so when those who had defended him left the OPC, Dr. Clark left as well. Because of the divisive actions of the WTS faction, one-third of the denomination walked out the door, including the OPC's largest congregation. That left the Van Tilians in control of the denomination, and they have been modifying it and history ever since. It is safe to say that had Machen lived, the Westminster faculty would not have sought to defrock Dr. Clark, and the OPC might have remained on a Biblical course for much longer than it did. As it is, the denomination is again confronted by a Seminary faculty that teaches error, this time on the doctrine of salvation, and their students and protegés are defending that error and their teachers from Church discipline.

In a letter to the editor of *The Calvin Forum*, in May 1947, Dr. Clark noted one of his critics' difficulty with stating the truth:

> In the April 1947 issue of *The Calvin Forum* on page 198, Mr. Edward Heerema says, "Men who take such a faulty and weak attitude toward the autonomous *will* of man that lies at the heart of Arminianism can be expected to have little trouble with Dr. Clark's notion of the autonomous *intellect* of man."
>
> Who these men are who hold to the autonomy of the will, I do not know. None of my friends hold such a view. But let them speak for themselves.
>
> What I wish particularly to make clear is that I do not and never have held to the autonomy of the intellect. Mr. Heerema's statement of my opinions is as far from the truth as it can possibly be.
>
> The unfortunate controversy [the Clark-Van Til controversy] about which Mr. Heerema writes would lose one of its unfortunate characteristics, if Mr. Heerema would determine what the truth is before he published his opinions.

Unfortunately, nearly 60 years later, neither the OPC Historian, nor the OPC denominational magazine, nor their defenders, have taken Dr. Clark's sound advice.

In another letter to the editor in the same issue, Floyd Hamilton, missionary to Korea, speaking for those defending Dr. Clark against the unprovoked assault by Westminster Seminary, had this to say:

> In the first place, we wish to assert our complete agreement with the doctrinal system of the Westminster Standards in the plain and obvious meaning. We disagree, however, with some of the inferences which the erstwhile complainants in the Clark Case made from certain parts of those standards. We accept the absolute authority of the Word of God and follow the grammatico-historical method of exegesis of the Bible. We disagree, however, with some of the exegeses made by these gentlemen, because we think that they are forced and unnatural interpretations of certain passages.
>
> In the second place, we deny any belief in "the autonomous will of man," and deny that either we or Dr. Clark hold or have held to any "notion of the autonomous intellect of man." Dr. Clark never "freely admitted...that he gets his definition of truth, not from exegetical considerations, but from 'common sense,' as Mr. Heerema asserted (p. 198 [April issue])....
>
> In the third place we deny that the "program of action" to which Mr. Heerema refers (p. 196) was antecedent to the Clark Case, and that its promoters set out to secure Dr. Clark's ordination in order to further that program. That program of action was never secret or underhand. So much has been made of it in the letters of Mr. Heerema that it is time it was published. It consisted of the following points, and was circulated among many ministers of the church in mimeographed form:
>
> 1. Preservation of the ideals that characterized our Church when it was formed in 1936, – namely, to be a spiritual succession to the Presbyterian Church in the U. S. A., actively to combat Modernism, and to engage in a program of aggressive evangelism; opposition to efforts working against these ideals, for example, agitation for exclusive use of Psalms, for

use of fermented wine in the Communion, for restricted or "closed" Communion, for subscription to the whole Confession of Faith by the laity as a condition of Church membership.

2. Appreciation of other Christian groups which stand for the Word of God, and readiness to cooperate with them in things of coinciding interest and concern.

3. A keeping alive of the Scriptural principles affirmed by the Rochester General Assembly (1942) in its statement on the expedient use of Christian liberty.

4. Recognition of the principle that the Church is of first consideration, and that organizations and agencies vitally and directly contributing to its life and work should be subordinated to it and supervised by it.

Our Church in instance after instance has been led away from these objectives, and it is high time the Church reset her course.

Specific Objectives

(In timely application of the above:)

1. The ordination of Dr. Gordon H. Clark.

2. Affiliation with the American Council of Christian Churches.

3. An official effort or deliverance against the Liquor traffic today.

4. Seek for Church supervision over Westminster Seminary and the Presbyterian Guardian.

(Notice that this was not an attempt by a group to control them.)

In his 1986 essay Hakkenberg incorrectly interpreted this program of action. Hamilton explained the origin of the document:

In considering this program the chronology is important. Dr. Clark applied for licensure and ordination in the early part of 1943. He was examined by the committee on candidates of the Philadelphia Presbytery that spring, and rejected by that committee. He was examined before the whole presbytery in an all-day meeting that lasted until late at night, and passed for licensure on March 20, 1944. He could not be licensed then because one-fourth of the members present protested his examination in theology, thus automatically holding up further action until his examination at a subsequent meeting, when only a majority vote would be needed to pass him in theology.

Now this "program of action" was first conceived by four ministers in consultation on April 18th [1944], a month after Clark had been passed for licensure by a large majority of presbytery. After sending out the first section in mimeographed form to a number of other ministers, suggestions were received, and it was put in final form, as quoted above, with the Specific Objectives added, on May 12th, 1944. Dr. Clark was licensed on July 7, 1944, and it was voted to ordain him at that meeting. He was ordained shortly afterward.

Mr. Heerema has put the cart before the horse in this matter. One of the factors that led to the formulation of the "program for action" was the determined opposition to Dr. Clark of the men who afterwards became the Complainants, at the March 20th, 1944 presbytery meeting.

As the man who first challenged the decision of the committee on candidates in the Philadelphia Presbytery to refuse licensure to Dr. Clark in the spring of 1943, I know what I am talking about when I say that neither I nor anyone else had any other motive in urging the licensure and ordination of Dr. Clark than that of seeing justice done to Dr. Clark. He had been one of the founders of our Church. He had just been dismissed from a certain chair of philosophy in a Christian college [Wheaton] because of his uncompromising advocacy of Calvinism in that institution. He had applied for licensure and ordination because he had an opportunity to become a pastor of an influential church if he were ordained. Having no doubt of his orthodoxy myself, I raised the matter in presbytery after the report of the committee on candidates had turned him down. It is an interesting fact that none of the issues afterwards raised in the Complaint was offered as a reason for his being turned down by the committee on candidates. As point

> after point regarding his beliefs was satisfactorily cleared up, and other questions raised, some of us began to wonder whether Dr. Clark would ever be satisfactory to the minority, many of whom afterwards became the "Complainants," no matter what his answers to questions might be.

Notice that Hamilton pointed out that "none of the issues afterwards raised in the Complaint against the ordination of Dr. Clark was offered as a reason for his being turned down by the committee on candidates." It seems that the WTS faction kept raising different objections, as each previous allegation was refuted, in a desperate attempt to prevent Dr. Clark from being ordained, and once he was ordained, to defrock him.

It is obvious that Dennison, Muether, and Hakkenberg misrepresented the "program of action." Presumably as historians they had read Hamilton's unrefuted account of the origin of the program of action. But instead of reporting this in their own writings, Dennison, Muether, and Hakkenberg set forth their own unsupported account of the origin of the program of action.

Unfortunately, this is not the only time, as I mentioned above, that history has suffered at the hands of OPC Historians. Even John Frame, defender of Van Til and Norman Shepherd, and adversary of Dr. Clark, once pointed out that the OPC version of the Clark-Van Til controversy gave the impression that Van Til won the controversy and Clark's ordination was overturned. Van Til's official biographer, William White, says as much: "The ultimate outcome of the controversy was that, for better or worse, the complaint [against Clark's ordination] carried."[19] It did not carry, and Dr. Clark's ordination was not overturned. White knew or should have known that. The most plausible explanation for these false-

19. William White, Jr., *Van Til: Defender of the Faith. An Authorized Biography*. Thomas Nelson Publishers, 1979, 128.

hoods are (1) bias against Dr. Clark and for Van Til; and (2) laziness and incompetence as historians.

To return to Muether's October 2004 *New Horizons* essay: Muether characterized Dr. Clark as a "pawn" of a sinister un-Reformed faction that wanted to take over the OPC and transform it into a "broadly evangelical" denomination. When I asked Muether about that characterization, Muether cited an essay by Hakkenberg and a book by Dennison, neither of which describe Dr. Clark as a "pawn" of anybody. There is no evidence in the sources Muether cites to support his description of Dr. Clark as a "pawn."

Finally, let us turn to the last source that Muether cited, Charles Dennison's *History for a Pilgrim People.* Muether cited in particular pages 131-135. On page 131, Dennison made a statement that seems to contradict Muether's innuendo that Dr. Clark was "broadly evangelical" and not Reformed: "It is unfair to say that those in the OPC who represented the evangelical cause in the 1940s lacked Reformed convictions and a specific commitment to a Reformed understanding of the church." So was Muether's statement inaccurate? It would seem so. But Dennison went on to say, "At the same time they had been influenced by the broad evangelical movement at many points." Unfortunately Dennison did not tell us who "they" are, nor did he document how "they" had been so "influenced," or what those "many points" were. Since this statement occurs in a section about Dr. Clark, however, one must presume Dennison included Dr. Clark in that nebulous "they." And that is simply a canard, unsupported by any evidence, and contradicted by the evidence we have.

But even Dennison did not call Dr. Clark a "pawn," as Muether did. Dennison did call him a "layman," which is false, for Dr. Clark was one of the founding Elders of the OPC in 1936. Dr. Clark had been ordained in the Presbyterian Church USA in the late 1920s, had brought charges against men who had signed the Auburn Affirmation, and had stood shoulder to shoulder with Machen in the formation and organization of the OPC, not only being present at the June 11, 1936, founding of the OPC, but also making the speech that nominated Machen as the church's first moderator. Dennison, as the official OPC Historian, tells us none of that history.

Dennison made another error of omission. He wrote: "No one at that assembly [the PCUSA Assembly of 1924] recorded a negative vote to this action [of the General Assembly to table the whole matter]. No one filed a protest. No one filed charges against any of the signers of the [Auburn] Affirmation in the time proximate to this decision, and therefore, within the prescribed statue of limitation" (48). All of which appears to be true. But what Dennison failed to mention was reported by Edwin Rian in *The Presbyterian Conflict*:

> One attempt was made to bring the Auburn Affirmationists to trial in the Presbytery of Philadelphia in October 1934, when the Rev. H. McAllister Griffiths and elders Murray Forst Thompson and Gordon H. Clark lodged six charges against eleven signers of the Affirmation in the Presbytery of Philadelphia for violation of their ordination vows. Through questionable methods and technical maneuvers the Affirmationists in the Presbytery succeeded in keeping the charges from being filed.... Yet the initiators of the charge felt morally obligated to start this suit in order to show the church that they regarded the signers of the Affirmation as heretics.

Rian went on to point out why these three men had not acted in 1924: "When the Auburn Affirmation was issued in 1923, Mr. Griffiths was not a minister of the Presbyterian Church in the USA and Messrs. Thompson and Clark were not elders" (51). Dennison omits this from his history.

Dennison's next paragraph on page 131 of *History for a Pilgrim People* is also misleading. Speaking of the so-called "program of action," Dennison wrote that "prior to that [OPC General] assembly [of 1944] four ministers...caucused for two days on the state of the church. They drafted a program for action and distributed it to a select group of men on May 11, five days before the assembly." Dennison stressed ("before," "prior to") that all this happened before the 1944 General Assembly to make it appear that these four ministers initiated the controversy and that Dr. Clark's ordination was the wedge they hoped to use to take over the denomination. But Dennison misled his readers, since he knew or should have known what really happened. Dennison's chronology misleads the reader into thinking that this "program" was drawn up before the Clark controversy began. But it was not. As both Floyd Hamilton and Hakkenberg explained, Dr. Clark had sought ordination in early 1943 and had been rejected by the committee on credentials and candidates in the Presbytery of Philadelphia. When some men in the Presbytery saw the vehemence with which the Westminster faculty opposed Dr. Clark, they came to Dr. Clark's defense. Far from the "program of action" being the start of the controversy and Dr. Clark's ordination the aim of some sinister conspiracy within the church, it was the ill-informed and vocal opposition to Dr. Clark's ordination that evoked the program of action. The program of action was developed a year after the WTS faction first opposed Dr. Clark's ordination. It was written by ministers in the OPC who believed that it was not in the Church's best interest to have the WTS faction decide who should or should not be ordained as ministers in the OPC. That is why the program of action included a provision to make Westminster Seminary answerable to the OPC. That is one reason the Westminster faculty opposed Dr. Clark so stubbornly. The OPC and its official Historians have misrepresented the causes, chronology, and nature of the controversy for decades.

In the course of his remarks, Dennison commented on the difference between Dr. Clark's view of revelation and Van Til's. He noted that "Truly, the 'incomprehensibility debate' is one of the great theological encounters in the twentieth century..." (133). This is a notably different assessment from Hakkenberg's description of the issues as "non-fundamental." Dennison accurately described Van Til's view as "Man's knowledge is like (analogous to) God's knowledge but it is not the same." This agnostic notion undermines all of Christianity, beginning with the doctrines of Scripture and propositional revelation. If the human words of Scripture are not also God's own divine words, then the Bible is a merely human book. If the truths revealed in Scripture are not what God really thinks, then we have no knowledge of God whatsoever, which is, of course, exactly what Herman Bavinck teaches in his systematic theology.[20] If man does not and cannot know what God knows, if there is and can be no identity of content between God's knowledge and man's, then man can know nothing, and we are all lost. On Van Til's view, Christianity must be a cruel hoax, for it claims to be a revelation of divine truth in human words.[21]

Dennison was candid about the reason Floyd Hamilton was not approved for a position at a Presbyterian seminary in Korea: "Floyd Hamilton was an able man but a defender of Clark and a determined evidentialist" (134). It was the WTS faction that opposed Hamilton, an "able man," and they opposed him because he defended Dr. Clark. Obviously the WTS

20. "This theory of God's incomprehensibility and of the unknowability of his being also became the point of departure and basic idea of Christian theology. God's revelation in creation and redemption fails to reveal him adequately.... Accordingly, adequate knowledge of God does not exist. There is no name that makes known unto us his being. No concept fully embraces him. No description does justice to him.... Justin Martyr calls God inexpressible, immovable, nameless. The words Father, God, Lord, are not real names but appellations derived from his good deeds and functions.... In a word, as says Athanasius, He is exalted above all being and above human thought.... Whatever we affirm in regard to him is true of him in a figurative sense only; hence, in reality he is not what we declare him to be" (Herman Bavinck, *The Doctrine of God*. The Banner of Truth Trust [1951] 1977).

21. For further reading on this point, see Gordon H. Clark, "The Bible as Truth," in *God's Hammer: The Bible and Its Critics*. The Trinity Foundation [1982] 1995.

faction was not going to seek the peace of the Church, but was spoiling for another fight. At that point, Dr. Clark's defenders left the denomination in disgust.[22]

Dennison, in those portions of his book in which he speaks accurately, does not support Muether's allegations. And Dennison's book is helpful in other respects. For example, he reminds us that Geerhardus Vos, Van Til's favorite teacher at Princeton Seminary and perhaps second only to Van Til in his influence over the contemporary leadership of the Orthodox Presbyterian Church, did not resign from the Princeton Seminary faculty when Machen did; he did not help Machen, Oswald Allis, and R. D. Wilson organize Westminster Seminary; he played no noticeable role in the Fundamentalist-Modernist controversy; and he never joined the OPC. Further, Vos adopted the discipline of Biblical Theology from the theological Liberals who invented the subject in the 19th century, including their completely un-Biblical premise: "the historical was first, then the theological." This Liberal subordination of theology to history, making doctrine secondary to and dependent on event, fits very well with the anti-intellectual character of modern thought and theology, but it does not fit well with Christianity. It is a denigration of Christian doctrine, and dressing this un-Biblical proposition up in conservative clothes cannot disguise its fundamental deformities.

Summary and Conclusion

The Orthodox Presbyterian Church may have a future as a Christian church, but only if it radically changes course. For decades its leaders have been promoting doctrines that are

22. Hart and Muether report that "The Committee on Foreign Missions, however, which included John Murray, was unwilling to send [Floyd] Hamilton [to teach in Korea] because of his advocacy and defense of Clark's views" (*Fighting the Good Fight*, 112).

false, opposed to Scripture and the Gospel. Now it is belatedly engaged in a struggle over the doctrine by which a church stands or falls, justification by faith alone. Many of its leaders do not understand that doctrine, which is why they failed to discipline both Norman Shepherd and John Kinnaird.

But the church gives no sign of changing course. After 60 years, its denominational magazine still genuflects before Van Til, and its official Historian still attacks Gordon Clark. As we have shown, that attack is false, scurrilous, and sinful. None of the statements demeaning Dr. Clark made by the official Historian of the OPC, John Muether, in the October 2004 issue of *New Horizons* is supported by the evidence.

1. Dr. Clark was not a rationalist, and neither OPC Historian Muether nor his source Van Til quoted any of Dr. Clark's words demonstrating that he was. The allegation is simply slander, repeated many times by disciples of Van Til, and now by the official Historian of the OPC. Further, to lump Gordon Clark and the Neo-orthodox theologian Karl Barth together in the same sentence, as Muether does when he accuses Clark of holding the "false principles" of "rationalism," appears to be malicious.

2. Nor was Dr. Clark a "pawn," as Muether stated, and none of the sources he cited support this slander.

3. Muether alleged that there was a faction in the OPC in the 1940s, a faction to which Dr. Clark belonged, that was "discontent with its Reformed identity." Neither he nor any of the sources he cited demonstrate this alleged discontent. Dr. Clark's 1943 essay, "An Appeal to Fundamentalists," demonstrates the falsity of Muether's allegation as it applies to Dr. Clark, who is Muether's target.

4. Muether's allegation that what was at stake in the controversy was whether the OPC's ecclesiology would be Evangelical or Reformed is also unsupported by any documentary evidence Muether cited. The ecclesiological issue in the controversy was whether the parachurch institution,

Westminster Seminary, would be subject to Church oversight. It was the WTS faction that opposed such ecclesiastical oversight, making them, not Dr. Clark, the advocates of an un-Reformed ecclesiology.

The official OPC Historian is not reporting history, but writing propaganda. Until the leaders of the OPC are willing to come to grips with history and acknowledge their errors of both teaching and practice, the denomination will continue its descent into apostasy. The leaders of the OPC have yet to acknowledge that they erred in handling the Norman Shepherd case. They refuse to acknowledge that they erred in handling the John Kinnaird case. If the 28,000 members of the OPC were to become informed and act on that information, perhaps the denomination could be saved. But most members of the OPC are not informed. Some who have become informed have protested the actions of the leaders of the OPC, and others who have become informed have left the OPC. The leaders of the OPC try to keep the members in the dark. To mention only one more example: The spokesman for the OPC Committee on Christian Education, Laurence C. Sibley, Jr., wrote a letter on behalf of the editors of *New Horizons* dated January 30, 1989, which says, in full: "We thank you for submitting a review of *Education Christianity, and the State* [by OPC founder J. Gresham Machen]. We have decided not to carry a review of this book and are returning your manuscript so that you may submit it to another magazine." Notice that Sibley did not merely decline to publish this review of Machen's book; he stated a general principle: "We have decided not to carry a review of this book." Not only have the editors of *New Horizons* refused to publish a review of a book written by its founder for the past 15 years, they have failed to publish any review or notice of any of the 60 books published by The Trinity Foundation during the past 25 years. Perhaps the leaders of the OPC are afraid that the members of the OPC might find out that Dr. Clark was neither a "rationalist," nor a "pawn," nor "broadly evangelical." Perhaps OPC leaders fear an informed membership because informed members might act to remove Teaching and Ruling Elders who teach error. It is this latter possibility that holds out the only hope, humanly speaking, that the Orthodox Presbyterian Church can be saved.

Reformation Day Declaration

We, the undersigned, urge all Christians to stand boldly against those who are not being "straightforward about the truth of the gospel" (*Galatians* 2:14).

We repudiate the expressions of the doctrine of justification contained in the North American documents "Evangelicals and Catholics Together" and "The Gift of Salvation," and the European document, "The Joint Declaration on the Doctrine of Justification," all written and endorsed by those who, in the interest of organizational unity, are willing to compromise between the Roman Church-State and the Reformation. In these documents Rome actually concedes nothing, while the Biblical and Reformed doctrine of justification by faith alone is either abandoned or ignored.

We reject the "New Perspective on Paul," advanced by writers such as James D. G. Dunn, E. P. Sanders, and N. T. Wright, that argues that Martin Luther and John Calvin at the time of the Reformation misunderstood what the Apostle Paul taught about justification and so constructed an erroneous and misleading doctrine of justification that Protestantism has unwittingly followed to this day.

We denounce the new perspective on covenant and salvation variously styled "Federal Vision," "covenantal nomism," "Neolegalism," and the "Auburn Avenue Theology." This theology, based on the false doctrine of Norman Shepherd and others, contradicts the doctrine of justification as enunciated by Scripture and the Reformed confessions. Instead of doing the honorable thing, that is, leaving their communions, many

Ministers and Elders in Reformed communions are perverting the Gospel and causing division within their communions with their false teaching that the Christian's justification is not by faith alone in the all-sufficient work of Jesus Christ, but is rather the eschatological result of the believer's lifelong faithfulness to Christ as seen in his imperfect works of obedience.

These teachers have rejected the clear Biblical teaching that justification is an act of God's free grace alone in which, forgiving believers of all their sins, He irrevocably imputes to them the perfect righteousness of his Son Jesus Christ as the ground of their justification. In no way do the imperfect works of the regenerate effect, augment, or change their justification before God. Justification is an act of God whereby He declares those for whom Christ died legally righteous forever the moment they place their faith in Christ. (See *John* 15:4-6, *Acts* 13:38-39; *Galatians* 2:16; *Romans* 1:16-17; 3:21-22, 28; 4:4-15; *2 Corinthians* 5:21; *Ephesians* 2:8-10; *1 Peter* 2:4-5.)

These teachers, either minimizing or denying the imputation of Christ's active obedience to believers, teach that justification is not a purely forensic declaration but a transforming activity in which the believer's obedience also plays a significant role. This false doctrine of justification includes within it the lie of Satan that Christ's righteousness is not sufficient for salvation and that an earned righteousness on the part of the believer is necessary for his justification before God.

For these reasons, it is necessary to protest and oppose this widespread false teaching within Reformed churches and to warn these errant Ministers and Elders, as the Apostle Paul declares, that those who would intermingle the believer's obedience with Christ's obedience as the ground or instrument of their final justification before God stand under God's own anathema (*Galatians* 1:8-9). They have made Christ's life and death of no value to them (*Galatians* 5:2), they have alienated themselves from Christ (*Galatians* 5:4a), they have annulled the grace of God (*Galatians* 2:21), and they have fallen away from grace (*Galatians* 3:10; 5:4b), because they are trusting in a "different gospel that is no gospel at all" (*Galatians* 1:6-7).

In order that what Christ said of the Philadelphians – you "have kept my word, and have not denied my name" (*Revelation* 3:8) – he may also say of us today; and

In order to preserve the doctrinal purity and unity of the Reformed churches; and

In order to urge these false teachers to remove themselves from their offices, or be removed by faithful Christians if they do not repent of their errors, we urge that all who love the one true Gospel of our Lord Jesus Christ join with us and sign this Reformation Day Declaration.

Adopted at Nottingham, Pennsylvania,
October 31, 2004.

Anyone who wishes to sign the Reformation Day Declaration may do so at The Trinity Foundation website, or by writing to The Trinity Foundation at Post Office Box 68, Unicoi, Tennessee 37692.

For a current list of signers, please visit The Trinity Foundation website, www.trinityfoundation.org.

About the Author

Dr. John W. Robbins received the A.B. from Grove City College at age 20, the M.A. in Political Theory at age 21 from The Johns Hopkins University, and the Ph.D. in Political Philosophy at age 24, also from The Johns Hopkins University. Since 1977 he has been President of The Trinity Foundation, publisher of Christian books and the monthly *Trinity Review.* He is the author and editor of hundreds of essays and several books, including *Ecclesiastical Megalomania: The Economic and Political Thought of the Roman Catholic Church*; *Without A Prayer: Ayn Rand and the Close of Her System*; and *The Church Effeminate.* A former chief of staff to a Member of Congress, Dr. Robbins has lectured at Harvard University, the University of Colorado, the University of Texas, Biola University, Chesapeake Seminary, Westminster Seminary, Sangre de Cristo Seminary, and the College of the Southwest.

Intellectual Ammunition

THE Trinity Foundation is committed to bringing every philosophical and theological thought captive to Christ. The books listed below are designed to accomplish that goal. They are written with two subordinate purposes: (1) to demolish all non-Christian claims to knowledge; and (2) to build a system of truth based upon the Bible alone.

Philosophy

Ancient Philosophy
Gordon H. Clark Trade paperback $24.95

This book covers the thousand years from the Pre-Socratics to Plotinus. It represents some of the early work of Dr. Clark – the work that made his academic reputation. It is an excellent college text.

Behaviorism and Christianity
Gordon H. Clark Trade paperback $5.95

Behaviorism is a critique of both secular and religious behaviorists. It includes chapters on John Watson, Edgar S. Singer, Jr., Gilbert Ryle, B. F. Skinner, and Donald MacKay. Clark's refutation of behaviorism and his argument for a Christian doctrine of man are unanswerable.

Christ and Civilization
John W. Robbins Trade paperback $3.95

Civilization as we know it is a result of the widespread proclamation and belief of the Gospel of justification by faith alone in the sixteenth century. Christ foretold this result in the Sermon on the Mount: "Seek first the Kingdom of God and his righteousness, and all these things will be added to you."

This brief overview of the history of western civilization makes it clear that our cultural debt is to the Gospel, not to Greece and Rome.

A Christian View of Men and Things Hardback $29.95
Gordon H. Clark Trade paperback $14.95

No other book achieves what *A Christian View* does: the presentation of Christianity as it applies to history, politics, ethics, science, religion, and epistemology. Dr. Clark's command of both worldly philosophy and Scripture is evident on every page, and the result is a breathtaking and invigorating challenge to the wisdom of this world. This is Volume 1 in *The Works of Gordon Haddon Clark.*

Clark Speaks from the Grave
Gordon H. Clark Trade paperback $3.95

Dr. Clark chides some of his critics for their failure to defend Christianity competently. *Clark Speaks* is a stimulating and illuminating discussion of the errors of contemporary apologists.

Ecclesiastical Megalomania: The Economic and Political Thought of the Roman Catholic Church
John W. Robbins Hardback $21.95

This detailed and thorough analysis and critique of the social teaching of the Roman Church-State is the only such book available by a Christian economist and political philosopher. The book's conclusions reveal the Roman Church-State to be an advocate of its own brand of faith-based fascism. *Ecclesiastical Megalomania* includes the complete text of the *Donation of Constantine* and Lorenzo Valla's exposé of the hoax.

Education, Christianity, and the State
J. Gresham Machen Trade paperback $10.95

Machen was one of the foremost educators, theologians, and defenders of Christianity in the twentieth century. The author of several scholarly books, Machen saw clearly that if Christianity is to survive and flourish, a system of Christian schools must be established. This collection of essays and speeches captures his thoughts on education over nearly three decades.

Essays on Ethics and Politics
Gordon H. Clark — Trade paperback $10.95

Dr. Clark's essays, written over the course of five decades, are a major statement of Christian ethics.

Gordon H. Clark: Personal Recollections
John W. Robbins, editor — Trade paperback $6.95

Friends of Dr. Clark have written their recollections of the man. Contributors include family members, colleagues, students, and friends such as Harold Lindsell, Carl Henry, Ronald Nash, and Anna Marie Hager.

Historiography: Secular and Religious
Gordon H. Clark — Trade paperback $13.95

In this masterful work, Dr. Clark applies his philosophy to the writing of history, examining all the major schools of historiography.

Language and Theology
Gordon H. Clark — Trade paperback $9.95

There were two main currents in twentieth-century philosophy – Language Philosophy and Existentialism. Both were hostile to Christianity. Dr. Clark disposes of Language Philosophy in this brilliant critique of Bertrand Russell, Ludwig Wittgenstein, Rudolf Carnap, A. J. Ayer, Langdon Gilkey, and others.

Logic
Gordon H. Clark Hardback $16.95

Written as a textbook for Christian schools, *Logic* is another unique book from Dr. Clark's pen. His presentation of the laws of thought, which must be followed if Scripture is to be understood correctly, and which are found in Scripture itself, is both clear and thorough. *Logic* is an indispensable book for the thinking Christian.

Lord God of Truth, Concerning the Teacher
Gordon H. Clark and
Aurelius Augustine Trade paperback $7.95

This essay by Dr. Clark summarizes many of the most telling arguments against empiricism and defends the Biblical teaching that we know God and truth immediately. The dialogue by Augustine is a refutation of empirical language philosophy.

The Philosophy of Science and Belief in God
Gordon H. Clark Trade paperback $8.95

In opposing the contemporary idolatry of science, Dr. Clark analyzes three major aspects of science: the problem of motion, Newtonian science, and modern theories of physics. His conclusion is that science, while it may be useful, is always false; and he demonstrates its falsity in numerous ways. Since science is always false, it can offer no alternative to the Bible and Christianity.

Religion, Reason and Revelation
Gordon H. Clark Trade paperback $10.95

One of Dr. Clark's apologetical masterpieces, *Religion, Reason and Revelation* has been praised for the clarity of its thought and language. It includes these chapters: Is Christianity a Religion? Faith and Reason; Inspiration and Language; Revelation and Morality; and God and Evil. It is must reading for all serious Christians.

The Scripturalism of Gordon H. Clark
W. Gary Crampton — Trade paperback $9.95

Dr. Crampton has written an introduction to the philosophy of Gordon H. Clark that is helpful to both beginners and advanced students of theology. This book includes a bibliography of Dr. Clark's works.

Thales to Dewey: A History of Philosophy — Hardback $29.95
Gordon H. Clark — Trade paperback $21.95

This is the best one-volume history of philosophy in print. This is Volume 3 in *The Works of Gordon Haddon Clark.*

Three Types of Religious Philosophy
Gordon H. Clark — Trade paperback $6.95

In this book on apologetics, Dr. Clark examines empiricism, rationalism, dogmatism, and contemporary irrationalism, which does not rise to the level of philosophy. He offers an answer to the question, "How can Christianity be defended before the world?"

William James and John Dewey
Gordon H. Clark — Trade paperback $8.95

William James and John Dewey are two of the most influential philosophers America has produced. Their philosophies of Instrumentalism and Pragmatism are hostile to Christianity, and Dr. Clark demolishes their arguments.

Without A Prayer: Ayn Rand and the Close of Her System
John W. Robbins Hardback $27.95

Ayn Rand has been a best-selling author since 1957. *Without A Prayer* discusses Objectivism's epistemology, theology, ethics, and politics in detail. Appendices include analyses of books by Leonard Peikoff and David Kelley, as well as several essays on Christianity and philosophy.

Theology

Against the Churches: The Trinity Review 1989-1998
John W. Robbins, editor Oversize hardback $39.95

This is the second volume of essays from *The Trinity Review*, covering its second ten years, 1989-1998. This volume, like the first, is fully indexed and is very useful in research and in the classroom. Authors include: Gordon Clark, John Robbins, Charles Hodge, J. C. Ryle, Horatius Bonar, and Robert L. Dabney.

Against the World: The Trinity Review 1978-1988
John W. Robbins, editor Oversize hardback $34.95

This is a clothbound collection of the essays published in *The Trinity Review* from 1978 to 1988, 70 in all. It is a valuable source of information and arguments explaining and defending Christianity.

The Atonement
Gordon H. Clark Trade paperback $8.95

In *The Atonement,* Dr. Clark discusses the covenants, the virgin birth and incarnation, federal headship and representation, the relationship between God's sovereignty and justice, and much more. He analyzes traditional views of the atonement and criticizes them in the light of Scripture alone.

The Biblical Doctrine of Man
Gordon H. Clark Trade paperback $6.95

Is man soul and body or soul, spirit, and body? What is the image of God? Is Adam's sin imputed to his children? Is evolution true? Are men totally depraved? What is the heart? These are some of the questions discussed and answered from Scripture in this book.

By Scripture Alone
W. Gary Crampton Trade paperback $12.95

This is a clear and thorough explanation of the Scriptural doctrine of Scripture and a refutation of the recent Romanist attack on Scripture as the Word of God.

Can the Orthodox Presbyterian Church Be Saved?
John W. Robbins Trade paperback $3.95

This small book, which demonstrates the central errors of OPC history and theology since the 1940s, is an alarm to awaken members of the OPC from their slumbers.

The Changing of the Guard
Mark W. Karlberg Trade paperback $3.95

This essay is a critical discussion of Westminster Seminary's anti-Reformational and un-Biblical teaching on the doctrine of justification. Dr. Karlberg exposes the doctrine of justification by faith and works – not *sola fide* – taught at Westminster Seminary for the past 25 years, by Professors Norman Shepherd, Richard Gaffin, John Frame, and others.

The Church Effeminate
John W. Robbins, editor Hardback $29.95

This is a collection of 39 essays by the best theologians of the church on the doctrine of the church: Martin

Luther, John Calvin, Benjamin Warfield, Gordon Clark, J.C. Ryle, and many more. The essays cover the structure, function, and purpose of the church.

The Clark-Van Til Controversy
Herman Hoeksema Trade paperback $7.95

This collection of essays by the founder of the Protestant Reformed Churches – essays written at the time of the Clark-Van Til controversy in the 1940s – is one of the best commentaries on those events in print.

Commentaries on Paul's Letters Hardback $29.95
Gordon H. Clark Trade paperback $21.95

This is Volume 12 of *The Works of Gordon Haddon Clark.* It combines his commentaries on *Colossians, Ephesians, First and Second Thessalonians,* and his essay *Logical Criticisms of Textual Criticism.*

A Companion to The Current Justification Controversy
John W. Robbins Trade paperback $9.95

This book includes documentary source material not available in *The Current Justification Controversy*, an essay tracing the origins and continuation of this controversy throughout American Presbyterian churches, and an essay on the New Perspective on Paul by Robert L. Reymond.

Cornelius Van Til: The Man and The Myth
John W. Robbins Trade paperback $2.45

The actual teachings of this eminent Philadelphia theologian have been obscured by the myths that surround him. This book penetrates those myths and criticizes Van Til's surprisingly unorthodox views of God and the Bible.

The Current Justification Controversy
O. Palmer Robertson Trade paperback $9.95

From 1975 to 1982 a controversy over justification raged within Westminster Theological Seminary and the Philadelphia Presbytery of the Orthodox Presbyterian Church. As a member of the faculties of both Westminster and Covenant Seminaries during this period, O. Palmer Robertson was an important participant in this controversy. This is his account of the controversy, vital background for understanding the defection from the Gospel that is now widespread in Presbyterian churches.

The Everlasting Righteousness
Horatius Bonar Trade paperback $8.95

Originally published in 1874, the language of Bonar's masterpiece on justification by faith alone has been updated and Americanized for easy reading and clear understanding. This is one of the best books ever written on justification.

God and Evil: The Problem Solved
Gordon H. Clark Trade paperback $5.95

This volume is Chapter 5 of *Religion, Reason and Revelation,* in which Dr. Clark presents his solution to the problem of evil.

God-Breathed: The Divine Inspiration of the Bible
Louis Gaussen Trade paperback $16.95

Gaussen, a nineteenth-century Swiss Reformed pastor, comments on hundreds of passages in which the Bible claims to be the Word of God. This is a massive defense of the doctrine of the plenary and verbal inspiration of Scripture.

God's Hammer: The Bible and Its Critics
Gordon H. Clark — Trade paperback $10.95

The starting point of Christianity, the doctrine on which all other doctrines depend, is "The Bible alone, and the Bible in its entirety, is the Word of God written, and, therefore, inerrant in the autographs." Over the centuries the opponents of Christianity, with Satanic shrewdness, have concentrated their attacks on the truthfulness and completeness of the Bible. In the twentieth century the attack was not so much in the fields of history and archaeology as in philosophy. Dr. Clark's brilliant defense of the complete truthfulness of the Bible is captured in this collection of eleven major essays.

The Holy Spirit
Gordon H. Clark — Trade paperback $8.95

This discussion of the third person of the Trinity is both concise and exact. Dr. Clark includes chapters on the work of the Spirit, sanctification, and Pentecostalism. This book is part of his multi-volume systematic theology that began appearing in print in 1985.

The Incarnation
Gordon H. Clark — Trade paperback $8.95

Who is Christ? The attack on the doctrine of the Incarnation in the nineteenth and twentieth centuries was vigorous, but the orthodox response was lame. Dr. Clark reconstructs the doctrine of the Incarnation, building and improving upon the Chalcedonian definition.

The Johannine Logos
Gordon H. Clark — Trade paperback $5.95

Dr. Clark analyzes the relationship between Christ, who is the truth, and the Bible. He explains why John used the same word to refer to both Christ and his teaching. Chapters deal with the Prologue to John's Gospel; *Logos* and *Rheemata*; Truth; and Saving Faith.

Justification by Faith Alone
Charles Hodge Trade paperback $10.95

Charles Hodge of Princeton Seminary was the best American theologian of the nineteenth century. Here, for the first time, are his two major essays on justification in one volume. This book is essential in defending the faith.

Karl Barth's Theological Method
Gordon H. Clark Trade paperback $18.95

Karl Barth's Theological Method is perhaps the best critique of the Neo-orthodox theologian Karl Barth ever written. Dr. Clark discusses Barth's view of revelation, language, and Scripture, focusing on his method of writing theology, rather than presenting a comprehensive analysis of the details of Barth's theology.

Logical Criticisms of Textual Criticism
Gordon H. Clark Trade paperback $3.25

Dr. Clark's acute mind enables him to demonstrate the inconsistencies, assumptions, and flights of fancy that characterize the science of New Testament criticism.

Not Reformed at All
Medievalism in "Reformed" Churches
John Robbins and Sean Gerety Trade paperback $9.95

This book is a response to and refutation of Douglas Wilson's book *"Reformed" is Not Enough: Recovering the Objectivity of the Covenant.* Wilson, one of the leading figures in the Neolegalist movement in Reformed and

Presbyterian circles, attacked covenant theology and proposed a "visible, photographable" covenant which one enters by ritual baptism, making one a Christian. Salvation received in this way can be lost by one's own lack of performance or by action of authorized representatives of the church. This refutation of Wilson is a defense of the Biblical Covenant of Grace.

Predestination
Gordon H. Clark — Trade paperback $10.95

Dr. Clark thoroughly discusses one of the most controversial and pervasive doctrines of the Bible: that God is, quite literally, Almighty. Free will, the origin of evil, God's omniscience, creation, and the new birth are all presented within a Scriptural framework. The objections of those who do not believe in Almighty God are considered and refuted. This edition also contains the text of the booklet, *Predestination in the Old Testament.*

Sanctification
Gordon H. Clark — Trade paperback $8.95

In this book, which is part of Dr. Clark's multi-volume systematic theology, he discusses historical theories of sanctification, the sacraments, and the Biblical doctrine of sanctification.

Study Guide to the Westminster Confession
W. Gary Crampton — Oversize paperback $10.95

This *Study Guide* can be used by individuals or classes. It contains a paragraph-by-paragraph summary of the *Westminster Confession,* and questions for the student to answer. Space for answers is provided. The *Guide* will be most beneficial when used in conjunction with Dr. Clark's *What Do Presbyterians Believe?*

A Theology of the Holy Spirit
Frederick Dale Bruner Trade paperback $16.95

First published in 1970, this book has been hailed by reviewers as "thorough," "fair," "comprehensive," "devastating," "the most significant book on the Holy Spirit," and "scholarly." Gordon Clark described this book in his own book *The Holy Spirit* as "a masterly and exceedingly well researched exposition of Pentecostalism. The documentation is superb, as is also his penetrating analysis of their non-scriptural and sometimes contradictory conclusions." Unfortunately, the book is marred by the author's sacramentalism.

The Trinity
Gordon H. Clark Trade paperback $8.95

Apart from the doctrine of Scripture, no teaching of the Bible is more fundamental than the doctrine of God. Dr. Clark's defense of the orthodox doctrine of the Trinity is a principal portion of his systematic theology. There are chapters on the Deity of Christ; Augustine; the Incomprehensibility of God; Bavinck and Van Til; and the Holy Spirit; among others.

What Calvin Says
W. Gary Crampton Trade paperback $10.95

This is a clear, readable, and thorough introduction to the theology of John Calvin.

What Do Presbyterians Believe?
Gordon H. Clark Trade paperback $10.95

This classic is the best commentary on the *Westminster Confession of Faith* ever written.

What Is Saving Faith?
Gordon H. Clark — Trade paperback $12.95

This is the combined edition of *Faith and Saving Faith* and *The Johannine Logos.* The views of the Roman Catholic Church, John Calvin, Thomas Manton, John Owen, Charles Hodge, and B. B. Warfield are discussed in this book. Is the object of faith a person or a proposition? Is faith more than belief? Is belief thinking with assent, as Augustine said? In a world chaotic with differing views of faith, Dr. Clark clearly explains the Biblical view of faith and saving faith.

In *The Johannine Logos*, Dr. Clark analyzes the relationship between Christ, who is the truth, and the Bible. He explains why John used the same word to refer to both Christ and his teaching. Chapters deal with the Prologue to John's Gospel; *Logos* and *Rheemata;* Truth; and Saving Faith.

Clark's Commentaries on the New Testament

Commentaries on Paul's Letters	Hardback	$29.95
(*Colossians, Ephesians, First*	Trade paperback	$21.95
and Second Thessalonians)		
First Corinthians	Trade paperback	$10.95
First John	Trade paperback	$10.95
New Heavens, New Earth		
(*First and Second Peter*)	Trade paperback	$10.95
The Pastoral Epistles	Hardback	$29.95
(1 and 2 *Timothy* and *Titus*)	Trade paperback	$14.95
Philippians	Trade paperback	$9.95

All of Clark's commentaries are expository, not technical, and are written for the Christian layman. His purpose is to explain the text clearly and accurately so that the Word of God will be thoroughly known by every Christian.

The Trinity Library

We will send you one copy of each of the books listed above for $500 (retail value $800), postpaid to any address in the U.S. You may also order the books you want individually on the order form on the next page. Because some of the books are in short supply, we must reserve the right to substitute others of equal or greater value in The Trinity Library. This special offer expires October 31, 2007.

Order Form

❑ Please add my name to your mailing list.
(You may also enter your email address at our website to receive special notices from The Foundation.)

❑ Please accept this gift for your work.
(All donations to The Trinity Foundation are tax-deductible to the fullest extent of the law.)

❑ Please send me _____ additional copies of *Can the Orthodox Presbyterian Church Be Saved?*

Our price schedule for *Can the Orthodox Presbyterian Church Be Saved?* is as follows:

1 copy $3.95
2-9 copies $3.00
10-49 copies.......... $2.00
100+ copies $1.00

Please add 15 percent shipping and handling per order within the U.S., and 20 percent per order outside the U.S.

Name ____

Address ______________________________________

____

Amount enclosed $ ____________________________

The Trinity Foundation
P. O. Box 68
Unicoi, Tennessee 37692

Website: http://www.trinityfoundation.org/